School's Out! Food's In!

School's Out! Food's In!

After-school food solutions from snack
attacks to super suppers

This edition published in 2011
LOVE FOOD is an imprint of Parragon Books Ltd

Parragon
Queen Street House
4 Queen Street
Bath BA1 IHE, UK

Copyright © Parragon Books Ltd 2007

ISBN: 978-1-4454-2420-0

Printed in China

Designed by Emily Lewis
Photography by Mike Cooper
Introduction written by Beverly Le Blanc
Recipe tips by Lorraine Turner
Food Styling by Sumi Glass (cover) and
Lincoln Jefferson (recipes)
Cover models: Carly Lou, Harry and Tilly Glass

NOTES FOR THE READER

This book uses metric and imperial measurements.
Follow the same units of measurement throughout;
do not mix metric and imperial. All spoon
measurements are level, unless otherwise stated:
teaspoons are assumed to be 5ml and tablespoons are
assumed to be 15ml. Unless otherwise stated, milk is
assumed to be whole, eggs and individual fruits such
as bananas are medium, and pepper is freshly ground
black pepper.

• Recipes using raw or very lightly cooked eggs should
be avoided by children, the elderly, pregnant women,
convalescents and anyone suffering from an illness.

• Sufferers from nut allergies should be aware that
some of the readymade ingredients in the recipes in this
book may contain nuts. Pregnant and breast-feeding
women are advised to avoid eating peanuts and peanut
products.

• Vegans should be aware that some of the readymade
ingredients in the recipes in this book may be derived
from animal products.

• Vegetarians should be aware that some of the
readymade ingredients in the recipes in this book may
contain meat or meat products.

Contents

Introduction

As every parent or carer knows, it is a challenge to get young school children to eat healthily. But it is a challenge worth accepting, because if they develop good eating habits at an early age, they will reap benefits throughout their adult lives.

The greater variety of foods your children eat every day, the more likely they are to get all the essential vitamins and minerals they need for their growing and developing bodies. And what your children eat when they come home hungry from school can have long-lasting effects. Try substituting Hummus with Crudités (see page 24) for a packet of crisps, and get your children into the habit of eating healthy snacks.

Eating Well for Life

High-profile campaigns have highlighted the important role a healthy diet plays in everything from children's overall health and behaviour to their concentration and performance in the classroom. Ideally, their diet – like your diet – should include plenty of fruit and vegetables, cereals, rice, pasta, bread and potatoes, with small amounts of lean meat, poultry, fish, eggs and pulses.

Foods high in fat, sugar and salt should only be eaten occasionally, and as youngsters' leisure time activities move from the playground to the computer, obesity is increasing at an alarming rate. Ways to counter this trend include offering water or milk instead of sweetened fizzy drinks, and fruit and vegetables rather than sugary biscuits and cakes – save those for occasional treats, rather than everyday snacks.

Yet actually getting kids to eat food that is good for them is easier said than done. Most children will choose a packet of crisps over crudités every day of the week, and school-aged children are notoriously fussy eaters. *School's out – food's in,* however, can help you achieve your goal with yummy, healthy recipes that make snacks and mealtimes pleasurable.

Strong Bones!

School-aged children need a variety of vitamins and minerals every day for optimum health, and calcium is a particularly important nutrient, as it is essential for healthy bones and teeth. Whole milk, yogurt and small amounts of cheese are all excellent sources. Or try desserts such as

Mini Strawberry Cheesecakes (see page 86) and Chocolate Mousse Pots (see page 94) – they will be hard to resist!

Go for 5

We are all encouraged to eat five portions of fruit and vegetables every day, because they are such a good source of vitamins, minerals and fibre. But as most parents know, getting children to eat one portion, let alone five, is not easy. You'll find imaginative ideas for incorporating vegetables into tasty main courses in 'The Vegetable Plot' chapter, beginning on page 52. And don't forget tempting yet healthy desserts, such as Fruit Skewers (see page 76).

Setting an Example

Always remember young children learn by copying adults, so the best way to encourage healthy eating is for you to choose the healthy options and set regular mealtimes. Mix and match recipes in the 'Making a Meal of it' and 'The Vegetable Plot' chapters, and the whole family will benefit.

1

Tuck Shop

Hearty Bean & Pasta Soup

4 tbsp olive oil
1 onion, finely chopped
1 celery stick, chopped
1 carrot, peeled and diced
1 bay leaf
1.2 litres/2 pints low-salt vegetable stock
400 g/14 oz canned chopped tomatoes
175 g/6 oz pasta shapes, such as farfalle, shells or twists
400 g/14 oz canned cannellini beans, drained and rinsed
salt and pepper
200 g/7 oz spinach or chard, thick stalks removed and shredded
40 g/1½ oz Parmesan cheese, finely grated

Serves 4

Heat the olive oil in a large, heavy-based saucepan. Add the onion, celery and carrot and cook over a medium heat for 8–10 minutes, stirring occasionally, until the vegetables have softened.

Add the bay leaf, stock and chopped tomatoes, then bring to the boil. Reduce the heat, cover and simmer for 15 minutes, or until the vegetables are just tender.

Add the pasta and beans, then bring the soup back to the boil and cook for 10 minutes, or until the pasta is just tender. Stir occasionally to prevent the pasta sticking to the bottom of the pan and burning.

Season to taste, add the spinach and cook for a further 2 minutes, or until tender. Serve, sprinkled with Parmesan cheese.

10/10 The carrots used in this soup help to promote good vision, especially night vision.

Creamy Tomato Soup

1 tbsp butter

½ red onion, minced

1 leek, chopped

1 garlic clove, crushed

1 carrot, peeled and grated

1 potato, peeled and grated

300 ml/10 fl oz low-salt vegetable stock

500 g/1 lb 2 oz ripe tomatoes, peeled, deseeded and chopped

1 tbsp tomato purée

salt and pepper

150 ml/5 fl oz full-fat milk

snipped chives, to garnish (optional)

granary rolls, to serve

Serves 4

Melt the butter in a large saucepan over a low heat and cook the onion, leek and garlic for 10 minutes, or until very soft but not browned.

Add the carrot and potato and cook for 5 minutes. Add the stock and bring up to simmering point.

Add the tomatoes and tomato purée and season to taste with salt and pepper. Simmer for 15 minutes until the vegetables are very soft. Add the milk and warm through, then transfer the soup to a blender or food processor and process until very smooth. You can pass the soup through a sieve at this stage, if you like.

Return the soup to the rinsed-out saucepan and reheat gently. Pour into warmed serving bowls and garnish the soup with the snipped chives, if desired. Serve with granary rolls.

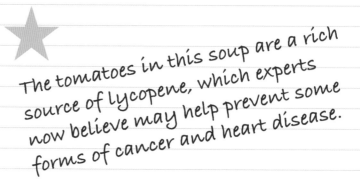

The tomatoes in this soup are a rich source of lycopene, which experts now believe may help prevent some forms of cancer and heart disease.

Tortillas with Tuna, Egg & Sweetcorn

1 large egg, hard-boiled
and cooled
200 g/7 oz canned tuna in
spring water, drained
200 g/7 oz canned
no-added-sugar sweetcorn
kernels, drained
2 wholemeal flour tortillas
1 punnet mustard cress

DRESSING

1 tbsp natural yogurt
1 tsp olive oil
½ tsp white wine vinegar
½ tsp Dijon mustard
pepper

Serves 2

To make the dressing, whisk the yogurt, oil, vinegar and mustard, and pepper to taste, in a jug until emulsified and smooth.

Shell the egg, separate the yolk and the white, then mash the yolk and chop the white finely. Mash the tuna with the egg and dressing, then mix in the sweetcorn.

Spread the filling equally over the 2 tortillas and sprinkle over the mustard cress. Fold in one end and roll up.

Tuna is full of protein, vitamins and omega-3 fatty acids, which can help lower blood pressure and cholesterol, and ease asthma complications. They are essential for the growth and development of young children.

Chicken & Apple Bites

1 apple, peeled, cored
and grated
2 skinless, boneless chicken
breasts, cut into chunks
½ red onion, finely
chopped
1 tbsp finely chopped
fresh parsley
50 g/1¾ oz fresh
wholemeal breadcrumbs
1 tbsp concentrated
chicken stock
wholemeal flour, for
coating
groundnut oil, for
shallow-frying

Makes 20

Spread the apple out on a clean tea towel and press out all the excess moisture.

Put the chicken, apple, onion, parsley, breadcrumbs and stock in a food processor and pulse briefly until well combined.

Spread the flour out on a plate. Divide the mixture into 20 mini portions, shape each portion into a ball and roll in the flour.

Heat a little oil in a non-stick frying pan over a medium heat and cook the balls for 5–8 minutes, or until golden brown all over and cooked through. Remove and drain on kitchen paper. Serve hot or cold.

Meat eaters can reduce the amount of fat in their meals, by eating more chicken. The leanest part is the chicken breast.

Chive Scrambled Eggs with Brioche

4 eggs

100 ml/3½ fl oz single cream

salt and pepper

2 tbsp snipped fresh chives, plus 4 whole fresh chives to garnish

25 g/1 oz butter

4 slices brioche loaf, lightly toasted

Serves 2

Break the eggs into a medium bowl and whisk gently with the cream. Season to taste with salt and pepper and add the snipped chives.

Melt the butter in a sauté pan and pour in the egg mixture. Leave to set slightly, then move the mixture towards the centre of the pan using a wooden spoon as the eggs begin to cook. Continue in this way until the eggs are cooked but still creamy.

Place the toasted brioche slices in the centre of 2 plates and spoon over the scrambled eggs. Serve immediately, garnished with whole chives.

You can ring the changes by replacing the brioche with toasted ciabatta, or why not boost your child's fibre intake with slices of freshly baked wholemeal bread?

Mini Pizzas

3 wholemeal English
muffins, halved

2 tbsp tomato purée

2 tbsp pesto

1 tbsp olive oil

½ red onion, thinly sliced

3 mushrooms, sliced

½ courgette, thinly sliced

2–3 slices ham or 6 slices
salami

100 g/3½ oz grated
Cheddar cheese or 6 slices
mozzarella cheese

Makes 6

Toast the muffins until golden, then leave to cool.

Mix the tomato purée and pesto together in a small bowl and spread equally over the muffin halves.

Heat the oil in a non-stick frying pan and then cook the onion, mushrooms and courgette until soft and beginning to brown.

Preheat the grill to high. Divide the vegetables between the muffins and top with the ham and then the cheese.

Cook under the grill for 3–4 minutes until the cheese is melted and browned. Serve hot or cold.

Why not try arranging the onion slices, along with some sweetcorn, olives or red pepper, into smiling faces on the pizzas? Just the thing to entice a fussy child to eat more vegetables!

Grilled Cheese Sandwich

1 stoneground buckwheat
boule loaf (about 17.5 cm/
7 inch diameter) or other
rustic round loaf
175 g/6 oz Cheddar
cheese, finely shaved or
coarsely grated
1 large avocado, halved,
stoned, peeled and sliced
2 tomatoes, halved and
cut into fine wedges
12 asparagus spears,
cooked, bottled or canned
4 slices Parma, Serrano or
Black Forest ham
pepper
olive oil

Serves 4

Slice the crusty top off the loaf; reserve for another use. Slice the loaf into two layers, making the bottom thicker. Place the bottom on a large piece of cooking foil.

Preheat the grill on the hottest setting. Toast the top surface of the top layer of the loaf until brown, then turn it and place on the foil.

Sprinkle 100 g/3¹/2 oz of cheese over both layers of bread. Arrange the avocado and tomato wedges on the bottom layer then sprinkle with half the remaining cheese. Top with the asparagus spears and ham, completely covering the edges of the ingredients underneath. Sprinkle with the remaining cheese and a trickle of olive oil.

Cook well away from the heat source for 3–5 minutes. Remove the plain cheese-topped layer first, when the cheese is bubbling. Cook the bottom layer until the cheese has melted and the ham is browned.

Cut the toasted cheese layer into 8 wedges and overlap them on the filling, alternating the plain and cheese sides up. Serve at once, cut into four wedges.

10 / 10 Excellent!

Hummus with Crudités

200 g/7 oz no-salt,
no-sugar canned
chickpeas, drained and
rinsed
½ garlic clove, crushed
3 tbsp tahini
freshly squeezed lemon
juice, to taste
1 tbsp natural yogurt
carrot sticks, red pepper
sticks, cucumber sticks
and apple wedges,
to serve

Makes 10 portions

Place the chickpeas in a blender with the garlic, tahini, lemon juice and yogurt. Blend until smooth.

Store in the refrigerator for up to 3 days and serve with carrot sticks, red pepper sticks, cucumber sticks and apple wedges.

The high fibre content found in chickpeas prevents blood sugar levels from rising too rapidly after a meal, making them an excellent choice for children with diabetes.

Avocado Dip with Spicy Potato Skins

4 large baking potatoes, scrubbed

3 tbsp olive oil

1 garlic clove, crushed

¼ tsp paprika

½ tsp dried chilli flakes (optional)

salt and pepper

2 ripe avocados, stoned and peeled

juice of ½ lemon

150 g/5½ oz soft goat's cheese

Serves 6–8

Preheat the oven to 190°C/375°F/Gas Mark 5. Rub the potatoes with 1 tablespoon of the oil, place on a baking sheet and bake in the preheated oven for 1–1½ hours, or until the flesh is soft.

Remove the potatoes from the oven, cut in half lengthways and carefully scoop out the flesh into a bowl, but leave a generous 1 cm/½ inch of the potato on the skins. You can use the potato flesh to make mash.

Cut the skins into wedges. Put the remaining oil in a large bowl with the garlic, paprika and chilli flakes, if using, and mix until well combined. Season sparingly with salt and pepper.

Toss the potato wedges in the spicy oil, spread out on the baking sheet and bake in the oven for 20 minutes until the skins are brown and crisp.

Meanwhile make the dip. In a separate bowl mash the avocado with the lemon juice, then mash in the cheese and a little of the potato flesh until well combined and smooth.

Serve the spicy skins warm, piled up, with little pots of the dip.

10/10

Cheese Twists

butter or margarine,
for greasing
85 g/3 oz Gruyère cheese,
grated
½ tsp paprika
375 g/13 oz ready-rolled
puff pastry, defrosted if
frozen
1 egg, beaten

Makes 20 twists

Preheat the oven to 200°C/400°F/Gas Mark 6. Grease a large baking sheet.

Mix together the Gruyère cheese and paprika and sprinkle over the sheet of puff pastry. Fold the puff pastry in half and roll out a little to seal the edges.

Cut the pastry into long 1-cm/1/2-inch wide strips, then cut each strip in half and gently twist. Place on the prepared baking sheet. Brush with the beaten egg and bake for 10–12 minutes, or until crisp and golden. Allow to cool on a wire rack.

10 / 10 You can give these twists a lovely smoked flavour simply by using a smoked cheese such as Applewood.

2/

Making a Meal of it

Sticky Drumsticks & Cucumber Salad

6 chicken drumsticks

2 tbsp maple syrup

2 tbsp low-salt soy sauce

1 tsp sesame oil

½ cucumber, thinly sliced

salt

2 spring onions, thinly sliced

Serves 6

Preheat the oven to 190°C/375°F/Gas Mark 5. Trim the chicken drumsticks of any excess skin and pat dry with kitchen paper.

Mix the maple syrup, soy sauce and sesame oil in a large bowl. Add the chicken drumsticks and toss well to coat.

Place the chicken drumsticks on a non-stick baking sheet and roast in the preheated oven for 30–40 minutes, basting occasionally, until the chicken is tender, well browned and sticky, and the juices run clear when a skewer is inserted into the thickest part of the meat.

Meanwhile, put the cucumber in a colander and sprinkle with a little salt. Leave for 10 minutes until the juices have drained out. Pat dry with kitchen paper and mix with the spring onions.

Serve the chicken hot or cold with the cucumber salad.

You can add other vegetables and salad to this dish, such as carrot batons. As well as adding variety, carrots are rich in vitamin A, which helps promote healthy bones, skin, hair, teeth and gums.

Home-made Chicken Nuggets

3 skinless, boneless chicken breasts
4 tbsp wholemeal plain flour
1 tbsp wheatgerm
½ tsp ground cumin
½ tsp ground coriander
pepper
1 egg, lightly beaten
2 tbsp olive oil

DIPPING SAUCE
100 g/3½ oz sunblush tomatoes
100 g/3½ oz fresh tomatoes, peeled, deseeded and chopped
2 tbsp mayonnaise

Serves 4

Preheat the oven to 190°C/375°F/Gas Mark 5. Cut the chicken breasts into 4-cm/1½-inch chunks. Mix the flour, wheatgerm, cumin, coriander, and pepper to taste, in a bowl, then divide in half and put on 2 separate plates. Put the beaten egg on a third plate.

Pour the oil into a baking tray and heat in the oven. Roll the chicken pieces in one plate of flour, shake to remove any excess, then roll in the egg and finally in the second plate of flour, again shaking off any excess flour. When all the nuggets are ready, remove the baking tray from the oven and toss the nuggets in the hot oil. Roast in the oven for 25–30 minutes until golden and crisp.

Meanwhile, to make the dipping sauce, put both kinds of tomatoes in a blender or food processor and process until smooth. Add the mayonnaise and process again until well combined.

Remove the nuggets from the oven and drain on kitchen paper. Serve with the dipping sauce.

Excellent!

Spaghetti Bolognese

350 g/12 oz spaghetti or
pasta of your choice

BOLOGNESE SAUCE
2 tbsp olive oil
1 onion, finely chopped
2 garlic cloves, finely
chopped
1 carrot, peeled and finely
chopped
85 g/3 oz mushrooms,
peeled and sliced or
chopped (optional)
1 tsp dried oregano
½ tsp dried thyme
1 bay leaf
280 g/10 oz lean mince
300 ml/10 fl oz stock
300 ml/10 fl oz passata
pepper
grated Parmesan cheese,
for sprinkling (optional)

Serves 4

To make the sauce, heat the oil in a heavy-based, non-stick saucepan. Add the onion and sauté, half covered, for 5 minutes, or until softened. Add the garlic, carrot and mushrooms, if using, and sauté for a further 3 minutes, stirring occasionally.

Add the herbs and mince to the pan and cook until the meat has browned, stirring regularly.

Add the stock and passata. Reduce the heat, season to taste and cook over a medium-low heat, half covered, for 15–20 minutes, or until the sauce has reduced and thickened. Remove the bay leaf.

Meanwhile, cook the pasta according to the instructions on the packet, until the pasta is tender. Drain well and mix together the pasta and sauce until the pasta is well coated. Serve immediately, sprinkled with the grated Parmesan cheese, if liked.

10/10 The proteins found in beef serve as an excellent energy source for active children.

Bacon, Pea & Potato Frittata

2–3 slices good-quality bacon

1½ tbsp olive oil

1 small onion, finely chopped

350 g/12 oz new potatoes, cooked, halved or quartered, if large

55 g/2 oz frozen petit pois

6 free range eggs, lightly beaten

salt and pepper

Serves 3–4

Preheat the grill to high. Grill the bacon until crisp. Allow to cool slightly, then cut into small pieces and set aside.

Heat the oil in a large heavy-based, ovenproof frying pan, add the onion and sauté for 5 minutes, or until softened and tender, stirring occasionally.

Add the potatoes and cook for a further 5 minutes, or until golden, stirring to prevent them sticking to the pan. Add the bacon pieces and peas, and spread the mixture evenly over the base of the pan.

Reheat the grill to high. Season the beaten eggs, then pour them carefully over the onion and potato mixture. Cook over a moderate heat for 5–6 minutes, or until the eggs are just set and the base of the frittata is lightly golden brown.

Place the pan under the grill and cook the top for 3 minutes, or until set and lightly golden. Serve the frittata warm or cold, cut into wedges or fingers.

As well as being an excellent after-school food, this frittata makes a tasty addition to school lunchboxes. You can vary the vegetables by replacing the petit pois with sweetcorn, chopped carrots or green beans.

Sausage & Bean Casserole

1 tbsp olive oil

8 lean pork sausages

1 onion, finely chopped

1 red pepper, deseeded and chopped

6 tomatoes, deseeded and chopped

1.2 kg/2 lb 10 oz canned no-salt-added mixed pulses, drained

600 ml/1 pint passata

1 tbsp chopped fresh parsley

1 tbsp tomato purée

salt and pepper

3 tbsp natural yogurt (optional)

Serves 4

Preheat the oven to 180°C/350°F/Gas Mark 4. Heat the oil in a non-stick frying pan and briefly brown the sausages. Remove from the pan with a slotted spoon and drain on kitchen paper. Add the onion and red pepper to the frying pan and cook until soft, then add the tomatoes and simmer for a further 2–3 minutes.

Add the pulses, passata, parsley, tomato purée and salt and pepper to taste and cook for 5 minutes.

Spoon the pulses and sauce into a casserole dish and add the sausages. Cover and cook in the preheated oven for 25 minutes.

Remove from the oven and serve hot with a swirl of yogurt, if liked.

✓ Peppers offer colourful protection against free radicals and are excellent sources of vitamin C and vitamin A.

Shepherd's Pie

2 tbsp olive oil

750 g/1 lb 10 oz lean fresh lamb mince

1 leek, chopped

1 small red onion, finely chopped

2 carrots, chopped

1 celery stick, chopped

100 g/3½ oz mushrooms, chopped

400 g/14 oz canned tomatoes

2 tbsp fresh thyme leaves

125 ml/4 fl oz water

salt and pepper

500 g/1 lb 2 oz potatoes, boiled and mashed

400 g/14 oz sweet potatoes, boiled and mashed

4 tbsp milk

knob of unsalted butter

Serves 4

Heat half the oil in a non-stick frying pan and cook the mince over a high heat, breaking it up with a wooden spoon, until well browned. Remove the mince from the pan with a slotted spoon, pour away any fat and wipe the pan with kitchen paper.

Add the remaining oil to the frying pan and cook the leek, onion, carrots and celery for 15 minutes until soft. Return the mince to the pan and add the mushrooms, tomatoes, thyme and water. Season to taste with salt and pepper and leave to simmer for 40 minutes, stirring occasionally.

Meanwhile, preheat the oven to 180°C/350°F/Gas Mark 4. Mix the 2 mashes of potatoes with half the milk and half the butter in a bowl and season to taste with salt and pepper.

Spoon the meat sauce into a baking dish and top with the potato mixture. Brush with the remaining milk and dot with the remaining butter. Bake in the preheated oven for 35 minutes until the topping is brown and crisp.

Lamb is an excellent source of protein, an essential building block for healthy children. To add variety, you can replace it with beef mince or soya mince, which are also rich in protein.

Sunny Rice

450 g/1 lb undyed smoked haddock or cod fillets

225 g/8 oz basmati rice, rinsed

450 ml/16 fl oz water

1 bay leaf

2 cloves

4 tbsp butter

55 g/2 oz frozen petit pois

1 tsp garam masala

½ tsp ground turmeric

pepper

2 tbsp chopped flat-leaf parsley

4 hard-boiled eggs, quartered

Serves 4

Put the haddock in a large frying pan and pour enough milk or water over the fish to just cover it. Poach the fish for 5 minutes or until cooked and opaque. Remove the haddock from the pan and flake the fish, carefully removing the skin and any bones. Discard the remainder of the poaching liquid.

Meanwhile, place the rice in a saucepan and cover with 450 ml/16 fl oz water then add the bay leaf and cloves. Bring to the boil, then reduce the heat and simmer, covered, for 15 minutes or until the water has been absorbed and the rice is tender. Discard the bay leaf and cloves. Set aside the covered pan.

Melt the butter over a gentle heat in the cleaned frying pan, then add the peas and cook for 2 minutes, or until tender. Stir in the garam masala and turmeric and cook for another minute.

Stir in the haddock and rice and mix well until they are coated in the spiced butter.

Season with pepper and heat through for 1–2 minutes. Stir in the parsley and top with the hard-boiled eggs just before serving.

Eggs contain a wealth of vitamins, minerals and protein. They are an excellent source of B vitamins and also include vitamin A – essential for normal growth and development.

Salmon Fishcakes

700 g/1 lb 9 oz skinless salmon fillet, cut into cubes

300 ml/10 fl oz milk

1 bay leaf

100 g/3½ oz broccoli, steamed until tender

700 g/1 lb 9 oz potatoes, boiled and mashed

2 tbsp finely chopped fresh parsley

4 tbsp wholemeal plain flour

pepper

1 egg yolk

2 large eggs, beaten

150 g/5½ oz fresh wholemeal breadcrumbs

2 tbsp olive oil

Makes 12

Preheat the oven to 200°C/400°F/Gas Mark 6. Put the salmon in a saucepan with the milk and bay leaf and bring slowly up to simmering point. Simmer for 2 minutes, then remove the saucepan from the heat, lift out and discard the bay leaf and leave the fish in the milk to cool. When cool, lift out the fish with a slotted spoon and place on kitchen paper to drain.

Flake the fish into a large bowl. Put the broccoli in a food processor and pulse until smooth. Add to the fish with the mashed potatoes, the parsley, 1 tablespoon of the flour, and pepper to taste. Add the egg yolk and mix well. If the mixture is a little dry, add some of the poaching milk; if too wet, add a little more flour.

Divide the mixture into 12 portions and shape each portion into a cake. Put the beaten eggs, remaining flour and the breadcrumbs on 3 separate plates. Roll each fishcake in the flour, then in the beaten egg, and then in the breadcrumbs to coat.

Heat the oil in a non-stick baking tin in the preheated oven for 5 minutes. Add the fishcakes and bake for 10 minutes, then carefully turn the fishcakes over and bake for a further 10 minutes.

The fish used in this recipe contains omega-3 fatty acids and will improve your child's concentration in class.

Pizza Fingers

PIZZA BASE

225 g/8 oz strong white
flour, sifted

1 tsp salt

½ tsp easy-blend yeast

150 ml/5 fl oz warm water

1 tbsp olive oil

TOMATO SAUCE

2 tsp olive oil, plus extra
for greasing and sprinkling

1 garlic clove, crushed

140 g/5 oz passata

½ tsp sugar

½ tsp dried oregano

salt and pepper

TOPPINGS

handful of cooked fresh
spinach leaves, tough
stalks removed, shredded
and squeezed dry

75 g/2¾ oz canned tuna in
oil, drained

½ yellow or orange pepper,
deseeded and finely sliced

4 slices salami

115 g/4 oz mozzarella
cheese

85 g/3 oz Cheddar cheese,
grated

Serves 2

To make the pizza base, place the flour, salt and yeast in a bowl. Make a well in the centre of the flour and add the water and oil, then mix with a knife until the mixture forms a soft dough.

Turn out onto a lightly floured work surface and knead for 5 minutes. Cover and leave for 5 minutes. Knead again for a further 5 minutes until the dough is elastic. Place in a lightly oiled bowl and cover with clingfilm. Leave in a warm place for 45 minutes or until doubled in size.

Preheat the oven to 220°C/425°F/Gas Mark 7. To make the tomato sauce, heat the oil in a heavy-based frying pan and fry the garlic for 1 minute, or until softened. Add the passata and sugar, then cook for 5–7 minutes, until reduced and thickened. Stir in the oregano and seasoning, then set aside.

Knead the risen dough lightly, then roll out to form a rough rectangle and place in an oiled rectangular tin. If you are not using a tin, place the base on a lightly oiled baking sheet and push up the edges of the dough to form a shallow rim.

Spoon the tomato mixture over the base. Top one quarter of the base with the cooked spinach, a second quarter with tuna, a third quarter with the yellow pepper and the remaining quarter with salami. Break the mozzarella cheese with your fingers and sprinkle it over the toppings. Sprinkle over the Cheddar cheese. Season and drizzle with a little olive oil.

Bake in the top of the oven for 12–15 minutes, until the topping is slightly crisp and golden. Slice into fingers before serving.

Home-made Fish Fingers & Sweet Potato Wedges

280 g/10 oz thick cod fillets, skin and bones removed

1-2 tablespoons flour, for dusting

1 tsp paprika

salt and pepper

fresh breadcrumbs or fine cornmeal, for coating

1 egg, beaten

sunflower oil, for frying

fresh peas or frozen peas, cooked, to serve

SWEET POTATO WEDGES

450 g/1 lb sweet potatoes, scrubbed and cut into wedges

1 tbsp olive oil

Makes 8–10 fingers

To make the potato wedges, preheat the oven to 200°C/400°F/Gas Mark 6.

Dry the sweet potato wedges on a clean tea towel. Place the oil in a roasting tin and heat for a few minutes in the oven. Arrange the potatoes in the tin and bake for 30–35 minutes, turning them halfway through, until tender and golden.

Meanwhile, cut the cod into strips about 2 cm/³/₄ inch wide.

Put 1–2 tablespoons flour onto a plate, add the paprika and season to taste. Put the breadcrumbs onto a second plate. Roll the cod strips in the seasoned flour until coated, shaking off any excess, then dip them in the beaten egg. Roll the cod strips in the breadcrumbs until evenly coated.

Heat enough oil to cover the base of a large, non-stick frying pan. Carefully arrange the fish fingers in the pan – you may have to cook them in batches – and fry them for 3–4 minutes on each side or until crisp and golden. Drain on kitchen paper before serving, if necessary.

Serve the fish fingers with the sweet potato wedges and peas.

Cod is low in fat and rich in iodine, an important energy-boosting mineral that will help improve your child's mental concentration. You can also use equally nutritious haddock in this dish.

3

The Vegetable Plot

Creamy Pasta Bake

175 g/6 oz wholewheat
pasta shells
1 tbsp olive oil
125 g/4½ oz button
mushrooms, quartered
1 broccoli head, broken
into small florets
1 tbsp cornflour
200 ml/7 fl oz milk
125 ml/4 fl oz half-fat
crème fraîche
salt and pepper
50 g/1¾ oz Cheddar
cheese, grated

Serves 4

Preheat the oven to 190°C/375°F/Gas Mark 5. Cook the wholewheat pasta shells in a large saucepan of boiling water for 10–12 minutes until just tender, then drain.

Meanwhile, heat the oil in a large frying pan and cook the mushrooms until beginning to brown. Boil or steam the broccoli until just cooked, then drain.

Blend the cornflour with a little milk in a jug, then gradually add the remaining milk, stirring constantly. Pour into the pan, add the crème fraîche and warm through, stirring.

Add the pasta and broccoli to the frying pan and season to taste with salt and pepper. Mix well, then transfer to a baking dish, top with the cheese and bake in the preheated oven for 15 minutes. Serve hot.

10

10 If your child does not like eating vegetables, pasta sauces are a great way to disguise them. Simply cook the broccoli, put it through a blender, then stir it into the sauce.

Spanish Omelette

200 g/7 oz new potatoes

1 tbsp olive oil

1 onion, thinly sliced

1 red pepper, deseeded
and thinly sliced

2 tomatoes, peeled,
deseeded and chopped

6 large eggs

1 tbsp milk

2 tbsp finely grated
Parmesan cheese

salt and pepper

Serves 6

Cook the potatoes in a saucepan of boiling water for 8–12 minutes until tender. Drain and leave to cool, then slice.

Heat the oil in an 18–20-cm/7–8-inch frying pan with a heatproof handle and cook the sliced onion and red pepper until soft. Add the tomatoes and cook for a further minute.

Add the potatoes to the pan and spread out evenly. Beat the eggs, milk, cheese and salt and pepper to taste in a bowl and pour over the potato mixture. Cook for 4–5 minutes until the eggs are set underneath.

Meanwhile, preheat the grill to high. Place the frying pan under the grill and cook the omelette for a further 3–4 minutes until the eggs are set completely.

Leave to cool, then cut into wedges.

Make this omelette fun by turning it into a fleet of boats. Make sails out of cocktail sticks and triangles of kitchen foil, cut the omelette into diamond shapes and stick a sail into each one.

Bean Burgers

400 g/14 oz canned
cannellini beans, drained
and rinsed
2 tbsp red pesto
75 g/2¾ oz fresh wholemeal
breadcrumbs
1 egg
salt and pepper
2 tbsp olive oil
½ small red onion, finely
chopped
1 garlic clove, crushed
6 granary rolls
6 tsp hummus
2 cherry tomatoes, sliced,
to serve
cucumber, sliced, to serve
green salad leaves,
to serve

Makes 6

Using a potato masher, mash the beans in a bowl until they are smooth, then add the pesto, breadcrumbs, egg, a pinch of salt and pepper, to taste, and mix well.

Heat half the oil in a non-stick frying pan over a low heat and cook the onion and garlic until soft. Add to the bean mixture and mix well.

Heat the remaining oil in the frying pan. Spoon in the bean mixture, in 6 separate mounds, then press each one down with the back of a spoon to form a burger.

Cook the burgers for 4–5 minutes, then carefully turn over and cook for a further 4–5 minutes until golden.

Meanwhile, slice the rolls in half and smear each one with the hummus.

Remove the burgers from the frying pan and drain on kitchen paper. Place each one in a roll, top with the tomatoes, cucumber and salad leaves and serve.

✔ Canned beans are quick to prepare, satisfying, nutritious, and children usually love them. Try using different varieties, such as haricot or black-eye beans, red kidney beans or chickpeas.

Roast Vegetable Lasagne

3 tbsp olive oil

4 courgettes, halved lengthways and thickly sliced

3 red peppers, deseeded and chopped

1 aubergine, chopped

2 red onions, chopped

5 shallots, peeled and quartered

250 g/9 oz button mushrooms

400 g/14 oz canned chopped tomatoes

1 tbsp tomato purée

50 g/1¾ oz butter

50 g/1¾ oz plain flour

600 ml /1 pint milk

salt and pepper

100 g/3½ oz Cheddar cheese, grated

200 g/7 oz fresh lasagne

2 tbsp grated Parmesan cheese

Serves 4

Preheat the oven to 190°C/375°F/Gas Mark 5. Put the oil in a large bowl, add the courgettes, peppers, aubergine, onions and shallots and toss well to coat.

Divide the vegetables between 2 baking trays and roast in the preheated oven for 30–40 minutes until soft and flecked with brown. Add the button mushrooms after 20 minutes.

Remove the vegetables from the oven and tip into a large bowl. Add the tomatoes and tomato purée and mix well.

Melt the butter in a saucepan over a low heat. Stir in the flour and cook, stirring constantly, for 2–3 minutes. Gradually add the milk and cook, continuing to stir constantly, until the sauce is thick and smooth. Season to taste with salt and pepper and stir in the Cheddar cheese.

Layer the vegetable mixture and sauce in an ovenproof dish with the lasagne, finishing with a layer of sauce. Sprinkle over the Parmesan cheese and bake in the oven for 30–35 minutes.

Remove from the oven and serve hot.

Most people now know that for optimum health we should be eating five portions of vegetables and/or fruit a day. This vegetable-packed lasagne will help your child to do it.

Spicy Rice Balls with Tomato Sauce

85 g/3 oz arborio rice
300 ml/10 fl oz vegetable
stock
1 tbsp olive oil
1 onion, finely chopped
2 garlic cloves, finely
chopped
1 tsp ground cumin
1 tsp ground coriander
½ tsp paprika
200 g/7 oz canned
chickpeas, drained and
rinsed
1 egg, beaten
fine cornmeal or polenta,
for coating
3–4 tbsp sesame seeds
sunflower oil, for frying

TOMATO SAUCE
1 tbsp olive oil
1 garlic clove, finely
chopped
400 g/14 oz passata
2 tsp tomato purée
½ tsp sugar
salt and pepper

Serves 4

Place the rice in a saucepan and cover with the stock, stirring well. Bring to the boil, then reduce the heat and simmer, covered, for 15–20 minutes, or until the water has been absorbed and the rice is tender. Remove from the heat, cover and let stand for 5 minutes. Drain and cool.

To make the tomato sauce, heat the oil in a heavy-based saucepan and sauté the garlic for 1 minute or until softened. Reduce the heat, add the passata, purée and sugar and season to taste. Cook until the sauce has reduced and thickened, then keep warm.

Meanwhile, make the rice balls. Heat the olive oil in a heavy-based frying pan. Add the onion and fry until softened. Add the garlic and spices and cook for 1 minute, stirring. Stir in the rice, chickpeas and the beaten egg. Transfer the mixture to a food processor and process until fairly smooth. Season to taste.

Put the cornmeal and sesame seeds onto a plate. Form all the mixture into walnut-sized balls and roll in the cornmeal and sesame seeds. Heat enough oil in a frying pan to cover its base and add the rice balls. Cook for 4 minutes, or until crisp and golden, turning occasionally. (You will have to cook the balls in batches.) Drain the rice balls on kitchen paper to mop up any excess oil. Serve immediately with the warm tomato sauce.

Crispy Vegetable Bake

25 g/1 oz butter, plus
extra for greasing
750 g/1 lb 10 oz potatoes,
thinly sliced
3 tbsp olive oil
1 garlic clove, crushed
1 tsp fresh oregano
leaves
1 large leek, shredded
2 parsnips, peeled and
grated
3 carrots, peeled and
grated
½ head celeriac, peeled
and grated
salt and pepper
200 g/7 oz feta cheese,
crumbled
4 eggs

Serves 4

Preheat the oven to 190°C/375°F/Gas Mark 5. Grease a 20-cm/8-inch round baking dish with butter.

Cook the potato slices in a large saucepan of boiling water for 5 minutes. Drain and cover with a clean tea towel to absorb the steam.

Melt half the butter with 1 tablespoon of the oil in a large frying pan and cook the garlic, oregano and leek for 3–4 minutes. Remove with a slotted spoon and transfer to a plate. Add the remaining oil to the frying pan and cook the parsnips, carrots and celeriac for 10 minutes until soft and cooked through. Season to taste with salt and pepper and cook for a further 5 minutes. Stir in the leek mixture.

Arrange half the potato slices in the bottom of the prepared dish, top with half the vegetable mixture and then sprinkle over half the cheese. Cover with the remaining vegetable mixture and cheese and top with the remaining potato slices. Dot with the remaining butter and bake in the preheated oven for 40 minutes until golden and crisp.

Five minutes before serving, poach the eggs. Serve the vegetable bake topped with the poached eggs.

Leeks belong to a vegetable family called the Allium vegetables. Garlic and onions also belong to this family.

Bubble & Squeak Patties

700 g/1 lb 9 oz potatoes,
peeled and cut into
even-sized pieces
300 g/10½ oz Savoy or
green cabbage, finely
shredded
1 tbsp olive oil
1 onion, finely chopped
1 tsp Dijon mustard
85 g/3 oz mature Cheddar
cheese, grated
1 egg, beaten
salt and pepper
flour, for dusting
vegetable oil, for frying

Serves 4

Cook the potatoes in salted boiling water for 15 minutes, or until tender. Drain well.

Meanwhile, steam the cabbage for 5–8 minutes, or until tender.

While the potatoes and cabbage are cooking, heat the oil in a heavy-based frying pan. Fry the onion for 5–8 minutes.

Place the potatoes and cabbage in a large bowl and mash using a potato masher. Add the onion, mustard, Cheddar, egg and seasoning and mix well with a wooden spoon until all the ingredients are combined. Leave until cool enough to handle.

Flour a large plate and your hands and shape the mixture into 8 patties. Heat enough oil to cover the base of a large frying pan and fry the patties in batches over a medium heat for 3–4 minutes on each side. Serve immediately.

Cabbage is not the most popular vegetable with children. However, inside these delicious patties, they won't even notice!

Easy Scone Pizzas

2 tbsp olive oil, plus extra
for oiling
1 onion, chopped
800 g/1 lb 12 oz canned
chopped tomatoes,
drained
1 tsp tomato purée
1 tbsp fresh thyme leaves
pepper
1 red pepper, deseeded
and thinly sliced
1 yellow pepper, deseeded
and thinly sliced
1 courgette, thinly sliced
250 g/9 oz baby spinach
leaves
200 g/7 oz wholemeal
plain flour
250 g/9 oz white plain
flour, plus extra for dusting
1 tsp demerara sugar
1 tsp bicarbonate of soda
1 tsp sea salt
350 ml/12 fl oz buttermilk
3 slices ham (optional),
chopped
250 g/9 oz mozzarella,
thinly sliced

Serves 6

Heat half the oil in a large frying pan and cook the onion for 5 minutes until soft but not browned. Add the tomatoes, tomato purée and thyme and season to taste with pepper. Simmer for 30 minutes until you have a thick sauce with almost no liquid. Remove from the frying pan and leave to cool.

Heat the remaining oil in the frying pan and cook the peppers and courgette for 5–8 minutes until just beginning to brown. Leave to cool.

Steam the spinach for 3 minutes or until tender. Squeeze out any excess water and chop.

Preheat the oven to 220°C/425°F/Gas Mark 7. Lightly oil 2 baking sheets. Put the flours, sugar, bicarbonate of soda and salt in a large bowl, add the buttermilk and mix well to form a dough. Turn out onto a floured work surface and knead briefly.

Divide the dough into 6 pieces, roll out each piece into a 13-cm/5-inch round and place on the prepared baking sheets. Spread the pizza bases with the tomato sauce, then top with the spinach, peppers, courgette, ham, if using and cheese. Bake in the preheated oven for 25 minutes.

Remove from the oven and serve.

You can use this recipe to make calzone instead of pizzas. Spread the topping over only half of each circle, fold it over into a half-moon, crimp the edges shut, then bake!

Chinese Noodles

250 g pack of tofu, drained
and cubed

salt

250 g/9 oz medium egg
noodles

1 tbsp peanut or
vegetable oil

1 red pepper, deseeded
and sliced

225 g/8 oz broccoli florets

175 g/6 oz baby sweetcorn,
halved lengthways

2–3 tbsp water

2 spring onions, finely
sliced

1 tbsp sesame seeds,
toasted (optional)

MARINADE

1 garlic clove, finely
chopped

2.5-cm/1-inch piece fresh
root ginger, peeled and
grated

1 tsp sesame oil

1 tbsp runny honey

2 tbsp dark soy sauce

Serves 4

Mix together the ingredients for the marinade in a shallow dish. Add the tofu and spoon the marinade over. Refrigerate for 1 hour to marinate, turning the tofu occasionally to allow the flavours to infuse.

Preheat the oven to 200°C/400°F/Gas Mark 6. Using a slotted spoon, remove the tofu from the marinade and reserve the liquid. Arrange the tofu on a baking sheet and roast for 20 minutes, turning occasionally, until the tofu pieces are golden and crisp on all sides.

Meanwhile, cook the noodles in plenty of salted boiling water according to the instructions on the packet, until the noodles are tender, then drain. Rinse the noodles under cold running water and drain again.

Heat a wok or heavy-based frying pan, then add the oil. Add the pepper, broccoli and sweetcorn and stir-fry, tossing and stirring continuously, over a medium-high heat for 5–8 minutes or until the vegetables have softened. Add the water and continue to stir-fry until the vegetables are just tender but remain slightly crunchy.

Stir in the marinade, noodles, tofu and spring onions and stir-fry until heated through. Serve sprinkled with sesame seeds, if using.

10 / 10 *Tofu is made from soya beans and is an excellent source of protein that is suitable for vegetarians.*

Pesto Potatoes

1 small baking potato,
scrubbed
handful of spinach leaves,
shredded
1 tbsp freshly grated
Cheddar or Parmesan
cheese

PESTO
25 g/1 oz fresh basil leaves
1 garlic clove, crushed
15 g/¾ oz pine kernels
4 tbsp olive oil
2 tbsp freshly grated
Parmesan cheese

Makes 1 portion

Preheat the oven to 200°C/400°F/Gas Mark 6. Bake the potato for 1–1½ hours, until tender.

To make the pesto, place the basil, garlic and pine kernels in a blender and process until finely chopped. Gradually add the olive oil and then the Parmesan cheese and blend to a coarse purée.

Steam the spinach for 3 minutes, or until tender. Squeeze out any excess water and chop. Preheat the grill to high.

Cut the potato in half and scoop out most of the flesh, reserving the skins. Put the potato flesh in a bowl with 2 tablespoons of pesto and the spinach and mash until combined. Spoon the pesto and potato mixture back into the potato skins and sprinkle with the Cheddar cheese.

Place the potatoes under a hot grill for a minute or two until the cheese is bubbling and golden.

10/10 Potatoes are high in antioxidants and are also a good source of vitamins B and C, potassium and iron.

4

The Naughty Corner!

Fruit Skewers

selection of fruit, such as
apricots, peaches, figs,
strawberries, mangoes,
pineapple, bananas, dates
and pawpaw, prepared
and cut into chunks
maple syrup
50 g/1¾ oz plain chocolate
(minimum 70% cocoa
solids), broken into chunks

Makes 4

Soak 4 bamboo skewers in water for at least 20 minutes.

Preheat the grill to high and line the grill pan with foil. Thread pieces of fruit onto each skewer. Brush the fruit with a little maple syrup.

Put the chocolate in a heatproof bowl, set the bowl over a saucepan of barely simmering water and heat until it is melted.

Meanwhile, cook the skewers under the preheated grill for 3 minutes, or until caramelized. Serve drizzled with a little of the melted chocolate, removing the fruit from the skewer if serving to younger children.

One of the benefits of pineapple is that it helps to build healthy bones. Pineapples are rich in manganese, a trace mineral that is needed for your body to build bone and connective tissues.

Sticky Fruit Flapjacks

175 g/6 oz unsalted butter, plus extra for greasing

3 tbsp clear honey

150 g/5½ oz demerara sugar

100 g/3½ oz no-added-sugar smooth peanut butter

225 g/8 oz porridge oats

50 g/1¾ oz ready-to-eat dried apricots, chopped

2 tbsp sunflower seeds

2 tbsp sesame seeds

Makes 16

Preheat the oven to 180°C/350°F/Gas Mark 4. Grease and line a 22-cm/8½-inch square baking tin.

Melt the butter, honey and sugar in a saucepan over a low heat. When the sugar has melted, add the peanut butter and stir until all the ingredients are well combined. Add all the remaining ingredients and mix well.

Press the mixture into the prepared tin and bake in the preheated oven for 20 minutes.

Remove from the oven and leave to cool in the tin, then cut into 16 squares.

Dried apricots are delicious, sweet and full of goodness for your child, including iron to prevent fatigue, potassium to aid clear thinking and magnesium for helping to relieve stress – ideal for homework and exams!

Apricot & Sunflower Seed Cookies

100 g/3½ oz unsalted butter, softened

50 g/1¾ oz demerara sugar

1 tbsp maple syrup

1 tbsp honey, plus extra for brushing

1 large egg, beaten

100 g/3½ oz white plain flour, plus extra for dusting

150 g/5½ oz wholemeal plain flour

1 tbsp oat bran

50 g/1¾ oz ground almonds

1 tsp ground cinnamon

75 g/2¾ oz ready-to-eat dried apricots, chopped

25 g/1 oz sunflower seeds

Makes 20

Beat the softened butter with the sugar in a large bowl until light and fluffy. Beat in the maple syrup and honey, then the egg.

Add the flours and oat bran, then the almonds and mix well. Add the cinnamon, apricots and seeds and, with floured hands, mix to a firm dough. Wrap in clingfilm and chill for 30 minutes.

Preheat the oven to 180°C/350°F/Gas Mark 4. Roll out the dough on a lightly floured work surface to 1 cm/1/2 inch thick. Using a 6-cm/2½-inch biscuit cutter, cut out 20 rounds, re-rolling the trimmings where possible, and place on a baking sheet. Brush with a little extra honey and bake in the preheated oven for 15 minutes until golden. Remove from the oven and leave to cool on a wire rack.

10/10 Add extra interest to these cookies by piping your child's name or initials in royal icing on the top of each one.

Cereal Fruit Cupcakes

100 g/3½ oz unsalted
butter

125 g/4½ oz clear honey

150 g/5½ oz porridge oats

50 g/1¾ oz unsweetened
crispy rice

1 tbsp sesame seeds

100 g/3½ oz mixed dried
fruit, such as pears,
mangos, apples and
cranberries, chopped

50 g/1¾ oz shelled pecan
nuts, chopped

Makes 12

Melt the butter and honey in a small saucepan over a low heat.

Mix the oats, crispy rice, sesame seeds, dried fruit and chopped nuts together in a bowl, add the melted butter and honey and stir to combine.

Spoon into 12 paper cake cases and press down well. Chill for 6 hours before serving.

✔ The porridge oats in these cupcakes are full of vitamin E, which supplies oxygen to help your child's endurance during sports, and soluble fibre, which is essential for healthy digestion.

Ice Cream Strawberry Sundae

8 scoops of good-quality
vanilla ice cream
25 g/1 oz chopped mixed
nuts, lightly toasted in a
dry frying pan
grated chocolate and
marshmallows, to serve

STRAWBERRY SAUCE
250 g/9 oz strawberries,
hulled and halved
2 tbsp freshly squeezed
orange juice
2 tbsp caster sugar

Serves 4

To make the sauce, put the strawberries in a blender with the orange juice and process until smooth. Transfer the mixture to a saucepan and add the sugar. Cook over a medium heat for 10–12 minutes, or until thickened. Leave to cool.

To serve, place a spoonful of the strawberry sauce in the bottom of a tall glass. Add two scoops of ice cream and another spoonful of fruit sauce. Sprinkle with the nuts and chocolate. Arrange the marshmallows on top. Repeat to make four sundaes.

10/10 Strawberries contain high levels of antioxidants. They also contain fibre which helps lower cholesterol and promotes a healthy digestive system.

Mini Strawberry Cheesecakes

75 g/2¾ oz unsalted butter

75 g/2¾ oz rolled oats

25 g/1 oz chopped hazelnuts

225 g/8 oz ricotta cheese

50 g/1¾ oz demerara sugar

finely grated rind of 1 lemon, and juice of ½ lemon

1 egg, plus 1 egg yolk

150 g/5½ oz cottage cheese

1 kiwi fruit

6 large strawberries

Makes 6

Line 6 holes of a muffin tin with muffin paper cases.

Melt the butter in a small saucepan over a low heat, then leave to cool. Put the oats in a food processor and pulse briefly to break them up, then tip into a bowl, add the nuts and melted butter and mix well. Divide the mixture between the paper cases and press down well. Chill for 30 minutes.

Preheat the oven to 150°C/300°F/Gas Mark 2. Beat the ricotta cheese with the sugar, and lemon rind and juice, in a bowl. Add the egg, egg yolk and cottage cheese and mix well. Spoon into the muffin cases and bake in the preheated oven for 30 minutes. Turn off the oven, but leave the cheesecakes in the oven until completely cold.

Peel and slice the kiwi fruit, and cut the strawberries in half. Remove the paper cases, top each cheesecake with the fruit and serve.

The kiwi fruits and strawberries in these cheesecakes are bursting with vitamin C, which helps your child fight off infections and speeds up the healing of cuts and grazes.

Blueberry Bran Muffins

150 g/5½ oz white plain flour

100 g/3½ oz light brown self-raising flour

1 tbsp oat bran

2 tsp baking powder

½ tsp bicarbonate of soda

pinch of salt

50 g/1¾ oz demerara sugar

1 tbsp clear honey

1 large egg

200 ml/7 fl oz buttermilk

150 g/5½ oz fresh blueberries

Makes 10

Preheat the oven to 180°C/350°F/Gas Mark 4. Line 10 holes of a muffin tin with muffin paper cases.

Mix the flours, bran, baking powder, bicarbonate of soda and salt together in a bowl and stir in the sugar. Whisk the honey, egg and buttermilk together in a jug.

Pour the wet ingredients into the dry and stir briefly to combine. Don't overmix – the mixture should still be a little lumpy. Fold in the blueberries.

Spoon the mixture into the paper cases and bake in the preheated oven for 20 minutes until risen and lightly browned.

Remove the muffins from the oven and leave to cool in the tin. Serve warm or cold.

Excellent! Oatmeal, oat bran and whole oat products are some of the best sources of soluble fibre. In addition to reducing the risk of heart disease, oat fibre can help control blood sugar, too.

Gingerbread People

175 g/6 oz plain flour

2 tsp ground ginger

½ tsp bicarbonate of soda

55 g/2 oz butter or
margarine

85 g/3 oz soft brown sugar

2 tbsp golden syrup

1 egg, beaten

TO DECORATE

Smarties and jelly orange
and lemon cake
decorations

**makes 6 people or more,
depending on the size
of the cutter**

Preheat the oven to 190°C/375°F/Gas Mark 5. Sift the flour, ginger and bicarbonate of soda into a large mixing bowl. Add the butter and rub into the flour with your fingertips until it resembles fine breadcrumbs. Mix in the sugar.

Warm the syrup in a small saucepan until runny, then add to the flour mixture with the beaten egg. Mix to form a soft dough, then knead lightly until smooth. If the dough is too sticky, add a little extra flour.

Roll out the dough on a lightly floured work surface then, using a cutter, make the gingerbread people. Place on a lightly greased baking sheet and cook for 10 minutes, or until just crisp and golden. Allow to cool.

Use the Smarties to make eyes and buttons, and attach the jelly orange and lemon cake decorations to make a mouth.

✔ Why stop at gingerbread people? Get your child to help you cut out other fancy biscuits using cutters of different shapes, such as hearts, trees and diamonds.

Orange & Banana Scones

sunflower oil, for oiling

150 g/5½ oz white self-raising flour, plus extra for dusting, and for rolling if needed

150 g/5½ oz light brown self-raising flour

1 tsp baking powder

½ tsp ground cinnamon

75 g/2¾ oz unsalted butter, diced and chilled

50 g/1¾ oz demerara sugar

150 ml/5 fl oz milk, plus extra for brushing

1 ripe banana, peeled and mashed

finely grated rind of 1 orange

150 g/5½ oz fresh raspberries, lightly mashed

Makes 12

Preheat the oven to 200°C/400°F/Gas Mark 6. Lightly oil a baking sheet.

Mix the flours, baking powder and cinnamon together in a large bowl, add the butter and rub in with your fingertips until the mixture resembles breadcrumbs. Stir in the sugar. Make a well in the middle and pour in the milk, add the banana and orange rind and mix to a soft dough. The dough will be quite wet.

Turn out the dough onto a lightly floured work surface and, adding a little more flour if needed, roll out to 2 cm/¾ inch thick. Using a 6-cm/2½-inch biscuit cutter, cut out 12 scones, re-rolling the trimmings where possible, and place them on the prepared baking sheet. Brush with milk and bake in the preheated oven for 10–12 minutes.

Remove from the oven and leave to cool slightly, then halve the scones and fill with the raspberries.

10/10 Bananas are a favourite for everyone, particularly children. They offer one of the best sources of potassium, which is an essential mineral for maintaining normal blood pressure and heart function.

Chocolate Mousse Pots

100 g/3½ oz plain
chocolate (minimum
70% cocoa solids), chopped
1 tbsp butter
2 large eggs, separated
1 tbsp maple syrup
2 tbsp Greek-style yogurt
100 g/3½ oz blueberries
1 tbsp water
25 g/1 oz white chocolate,
grated

Makes 6

Put the chocolate and butter in a heatproof bowl, set the bowl over a saucepan of barely simmering water and heat until melted. Leave to cool slightly, then stir in the egg yolks, maple syrup and yogurt.

Whisk the egg whites in a large, grease-free bowl until stiff, then fold into the chocolate mixture. Divide between 6 small ramekins and chill for 4 hours.

Meanwhile, put the blueberries in a small saucepan with the water and cook until the berries begin to pop and turn glossy. Leave to cool, then chill.

To serve, top each mousse with a few blueberries and a little white chocolate.

Yogurt is not only delicious, but has great health benefits. It is an excellent source of protein, calcium, riboflavin and vitamin B 12. When compared with milk, yogurt contains more calcium and protein because of the added cultures in the yogurt.

Index